AF576933

# A Nuisance of Cats

# A Nuisance of Cats

## The Curious Collective

NON-ARTWORK: hc fargot
ARTWORK: wrolf bronesby

PUBLISHED BY

LITTLE KNOWN SCHOOL PRESS

A DIVISION OF COLD HARD SOFTWARE INC.

WWW.LITTLEKNOWNSCHOOLPRESS.COM

ISBN: 978-0-9825150-1-3

FIRST EDITION

PRINTED IN CHINA

FOR ALICE AND RAUSCH

Time spent with cats is never wasted.

Sigmund Freud

A is for Astro aglow in a tree

B is for Brownie baked in a brie

C is for Clinton chasing some tail

D is for Dahlia debating a snail

E is for Einstein eyeing some eggs

F is for Fluffy feasting on legs

G is for Greystoke grooming his pride

H is for Harlow hitching a ride

I is for Iggy into the fish

J is for Josie juking a dish

K is for Kafka killing some time

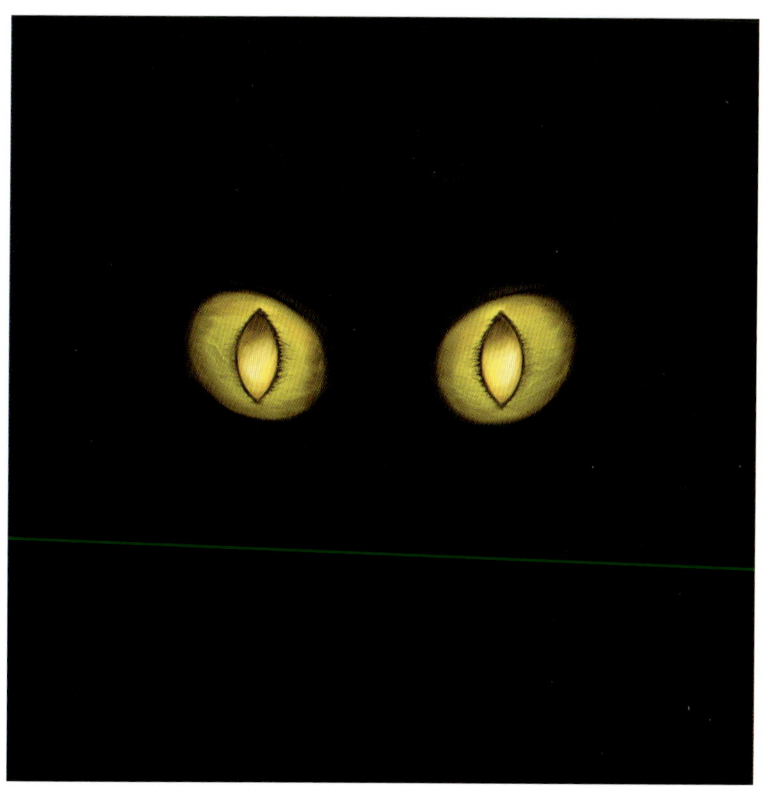

L is for Lemon lurking sublime

M is for Mickey making a mouse

N is for Nadia kneading her spouse

O is for Orson observing a fox

P is for Pandora packed in a box

Q is for Quincy quick on his feet

R is for Ripley ripping a seat

S is for Sascha stalking his prey

T is for Taylor tailing a jay

U is for Urlacher under the stairs

V is for Vixen viewing da bears

W is for Wiley wrecking a ball

X is for X-Ray examining all

Y is for Yuri yielding the floor

Z is for Zoe zoned to the core

a litter of kittens